RESCUE 911™

AMAZING RESCUES

BY ALISON HENDRIE

BDD SPECIAL

The stories in this book are based on actual events as depicted on RESCUE 911.

If 911 isn't the emergency number in your area, learn the emergency numbers used where you live, and post them by each phone.

**Special Thanks to
Arnold Shapiro Productions**

Published by The Trumpet Club
1540 Broadway, New York, New York 10036
Text copyright © 1993 by The Trumpet Club, Inc.

ISBN: 0-440-40909-8

Produced by Neuwirth & Associates, Inc.

Printed in the United States of America
April 1993

1 3 5 7 9 10 8 6 4 2
OPM

Contents

☆ ☆ ☆

Introduction

☆ ☆ ☆

Life is a funny thing. What may start out as a boring day could suddenly, unexpectedly become a horrifying, split-second duel with death. In the blink of an eye, a lazy afternoon could erupt into a quest for survival.

Amazingly, life can sometimes throw us the kind of surprises you think are only in the movies. Sure, *Home Alone*™ is chock-full of crazy pranks and strange events, with the young hero thinking fast and staging and enduring all kinds of wild escapades and escapes. But that's just the movies, right? Wrong.

Every week, you can see for yourselves the kinds of amazing, dangerous and life-threatening events that happen to everyday people — people like you and me.

Rescue 911, the national TV show, brings real-life

1

heroes into your own home, telling their hard-to-believe but true stories of adventure and danger and recreating them in front of your very eyes. But just like in the movies, some adventures are more amazing than others.

Sometimes, emergencies can happen where there is no help nearby — no phone, even — or in places you would never expect. Sometimes even the heroes are not quite who or what you would expect.

A parrot who saves an entire family? A dog out-witting a poisonous snake? Yes. On the next pages, you'll read about these and other real-life heroes brought together by life-threatening occurrences.

Amazing.

☆☆☆

Saved by the Bird

★ ★ ☆

People and animals have a lot in common. They both eat, sleep, and breathe. But there are a lot of differences between them, and those differences are part of what makes us wonder about and enjoy animals so much. There is much we don't know, and there is really no way to communicate with the animal kingdom in the way we communicate with our friends and families.

Birds, especially, seem so unusual, doing things we could never do. Soaring among the clouds, birds seem to be completely free ... no boundaries, just bird and sky, wings and wind.

As a pet, a bird can give us beauty and song and friendship. Using our imaginations, we can dream of the places a bird has flown, wondering what it must be like to look down on the earth with a bird's-eye view.

A parrot, in particular, is a fascinating pet. How exciting to think that you can talk to your bird — and that it can talk back to you, in your own language! Of course, not all parrots can talk. But they do have their own way of communicating with people when they need to. For example, meet Elliott, a parrot who was not too swift with conversation, but whose friendship and bravery saved the lives of the people he lived with — his human family. Elliott the Parrot freed his family, the Ascolillos, from certain death.

The Ascolillos met their pet Elliott in an ususual way. The year was 1982. One chilly autumn day in Boston, Massachusetts, Ed and Irene Ascolillo watched with delight as a blue-fronted Amazon parrot flitted among the fall leaves near their house. A parrot roaming free in the city of Boston was a surprising sight, and the entire Ascolillo family watched its every move. Seven-year-old Eddie, Jr., and six-year-old Michael joined their parents in trying to catch the elusive parrot, enjoying diving and swooping after the beautiful bird. Each time they thought they had grabbed him, they ended up with a handful of air. The bird just wouldn't be caught. This reminded the boys of their favorite movie, *E.T.*, and so they soon began calling the parrot "Elliott."

The Ascolillos never gave up. They left birdseed on a blanket outside their door and would often watch silently as their feathered friend munched happily. But before they could reach out to capture him, off he would fly, leaving Ed and Irene flustered but smiling.

One icy December evening, so cold that the entire neighborhood stayed bundled up inside the warmth of their homes, the Ascolillo family discovered their precious parrot frozen still on the blanket. Gently, they lifted him inside. This time, Elliott did not protest or try to escape. He looked hurt and hungry but not too scared. He seemed to sense that these people would help him. And he was right.

After a visit with the veterinarian — a doctor who treats sick animals — they discovered that Elliott's feet were frostbitten. This can happen to anyone, humans and animals alike, if they are out in the cold too long. The cold, or frost, gets into the tissue inside the skin — fingers and toes are usually more susceptible to the cold — and the frost will damage this tissue, sometimes, as in Elliott's case, very badly. Elliott's feet were so bad that he soon lost all of his toes and had only stumps for feet.

But the bird was alive and, other than his feet, seemed just fine. He was adopted by the Ascolillos and was soon a part of the family. Often, when a bird is brought indoors to live, his wings are clipped, or trimmed, so he doesn't fly around and hurt himself. Ed and Irene knew it was difficult for Elliott to walk, so they decided to leave his wings alone and allow him to fly whenever he wanted.

Elliott was given his own room on the second

Elliott the Parrot may have had frostbitten stumps for feet, but he was a beloved member of the family.

floor of the house, next to the boys' bedroom, and he settled in to his new life quickly and easily. Elliott was an Ascolillo now, and he sure seemed to like it. As time went by, the family grew closer to him, and although Elliott never did learn to actually talk as some parrots do, he could communicate with the family and they with him.

It was just about a year after the Ascolillos first discovered Elliott flying outside their home that Elliott's ability to communicate was put to the test. And his passing the test meant life or death for the Ascolillo family.

September 23, 1983, was the busiest night in the history of the Boston Fire Department. A major water-main break in the section of town where the

Ascolillos lived kept fire fighters jumping all night.
The break caused a gas regulator to stop working,
which flooded the whole neighborhood's gas system
with a surge of gas. This kind of gas, used to heat
homes and light stoves, was now flowing uncon-
trollably through the Ascolillo neighborhood. The
gas was very flammable, which means it could
catch fire easily. With this kind of major gas leak,
the entire neighborhood — complete with houses
and people — could be blown sky-high at any
moment.

Police and fire fighters were on the scene immediately, driving through the streets and waking
people up with announcements over their loud-
speakers. The neighbors were warned to turn off
their gas and not to turn on the lights. They were
told to get out of their homes right away. The
streets were soon filling with sleepy but scared
families.

Down the block, Ed and Irene were sleeping
soundly and comfortably in their third-floor bedroom. On the floor below, Eddie, Jr., and Michael
were also fast asleep, dreaming peacefully. They
had no idea what danger was in their own home.
They could not hear the police announcements.
They did not know that if they stayed asleep, they
might never wake up.

Elliott, however, was very much awake.

Soaring into action, the bird was about to save
his newfound family, just as they had saved him
from death only a year before. Elliott flapped his

wings mightily as he raced from his second-floor
room, up the stairs to the third-floor bedroom of Ed
and Irene. Although the bird had never ventured
upstairs, he seemed to know exactly where to go
and what to do. Swooping and beating the air with
his wings, Elliott tried desperately to wake the
sleeping couple. And though Elliott had never been
able to talk, he did begin to make screeching and
squawking noises in a cry for help.

Meanwhile, out on the street the neighborhood
seemed like a battle zone. People were running out
of their houses wearing only their pajamas, trying
to help one another while fire fighters and police
officers called out for everyone to evacuate — or
leave — their homes. By now it was three in the
morning and very dark, but it could have been the
middle of the day for all the activity in the streets.

Three major fires blazed at the same time, and
fire fighters and rescuers fought long and hard to
keep them under control. Also, several smaller
fires and flare-ups broke out, and there was a gen-
eral feeling that this was not real, this couldn't be
happening.

Back in the Ascolillo house, Elliott was increas-
ing his flapping and screeching until, finally, his
efforts paid off.

Blinking and yawning, Ed slowly sat up in bed,
still not understanding what was happening. When
he saw Elliott in such a frenzy, he thought he must
still be dreaming. Was this the quiet, loving little

bird who never made a peep? What was wrong? What did Elliott want?

Struggling to awaken his wife Irene, Ed shook off the last feelings of sleep and finally sniffed the air. Gas. Ed could smell gas throughout the house. He knew that the smell was a sign of danger and that he must get his family out of the house quickly or there could be serious trouble. Irene was still groggy from sleep, but soon realized the danger and, together with Ed, rushed to their sons' room.

Eddie, Jr., and Michael were sleeping and felt cold and clammy. Ed and Irene did not know if they were just very tired or if the gas had already made them sick. Breathing in too much gas can make you lose consciousness, cause you to become very ill, and even kill you. So, of course, Ed and Irene grabbed the children from their beds and raced out of the house as fast as possible. They were careful not to turn on the lights because they knew even one small spark from a light switch could set off an explosion and blow up the house.

Safely outside, the Ascolillos saw all the commotion, heard the wailing of fire trucks and the cries of their friends and neighbors. They were surprised that they had slept through all this activity and were grateful to Elliott for saving their lives. They looked around to thank him — but where was he? Elliott must still be in the house!

Without a second thought, Ed ran back into the gas-filled house — a house that could explode any minute — to rescue his hero bird. Calling to Elliott, Ed was able to get the frightened parrot into his cage and to the safety of his family waiting outside. Irene walked the boys and Elliott to Ed's mother's home only a few blocks away.

It was a warm evening, and most local homeowners had left their windows open to let in fresh air. The Ascolillos, however, had kept theirs shut. The gas in the house could not escape, and soon there was a dangerously high level of gas that was building every minute.

For the second time that night, Ed bravely dashed into his home, this time to open the windows and let out all the gas. Irene and neighbors all called out to Ed, urging him to get out of the house before it was too late.

Racing through the rooms to open the windows, Ed knew he was in danger. But he also knew he wanted to save his house from destruction, so he went down to the basement to turn off the house's main gas valve. The smell was especially strong down there and it was difficult to breathe. Ed strained to turn off the gas valve, but it seemed stuck and wouldn't budge. He put all his strength into it, and suddenly the valve moved. He had turned off the gas and was ready to leave when, behind him, came an explosion.

Flames leaped out at him from the hot-water heater. With gas still lingering in the house, a small fire could turn into an inferno in seconds. Thinking fast, Ed grabbed a fire extinguisher next to the furnace and blasted the flames. The fire was soon out, and, coughing and choking, Ed made his way back outside to his waiting wife and friends.

The Ascolillo family was reunited, along with Elliott, and their home remained safe and secure. Although fire fighters worked tirelessly through the night as several fires continued to flare, the neighborhood was returned to normal in a matter of days. Incredibly, and thanks to the professional work of rescuers, police, and fire fighters, not one person died in the ordeal.

Elliott was truly an amazing hero, and the Ascolillos are closer to him than ever before. Dr. McMillan, the veterinarian, was also very impressed with Elliott's story. She explained to the family that birds kept in captivity, such as in a house, are known to treat the people around them like other birds — like their own family. In all families, human or not, the members' safety is a major concern. Elliott, sensing danger, warned the Ascolillo family as if he were warning his own bird family in the only way he knew how — by flapping and making noise to alert them to the problem.

Elliott was a hero. In 1987, he was awarded the highest honor for an animal: the Pet of the Year Award of the Massachusetts SPCA. Elliott won the award from a field of over 2,500 other pets — and became the first bird ever to win this unique honor.

☆☆☆

Amazing Facts

Did you know:

- Parrots are the most beloved bird pet. They are best known for their ability to imitate human sound — even talk!

- Parrots live to be a half-century old. Some even live longer!

- Parrots are very smart and can learn fast. Some parrots have learned to count to seven, and most can figure out a simple lock on a cage. So watch out for parrots on the loose!

- Parrots are affectionate creatures with humans and like to be stroked and petted — just like dogs.

★★★

Hanging Hang Glider

☆ ☆ ☆

Imagine holding out your arms, running across the grass, and suddenly taking off and flying up through the clouds. There you are, soaring around with the birds, looking down at your friends and your mom and dad on the ground like tiny little ants at a picnic. With the wind in your hair and the sun on your face, you would forget your troubles — like homework and big brothers — and just float above it all.

You might have flown in an airplane before, but as you know, that isn't quite the same. Airplanes carry too many people, and you don't always get to sit near a window. A helicopter has a better view, but it makes too much noise and would scare away the birds. What could be the best way to take to the sky and fly like you do in your dreams?

Hang gliding. Light, graceful, colorful. Hang

gliders are like giant wings that attach directly to
the body, taking people into the sky without motors
or metal. Made of simple kite-like wings, with a
crossbar to hold on to, the hang glider lifts the flier,
or pilot, up to the sky, with the help of the wind.
And although the pilot is strapped onto the equipment, there are no seats or platforms to sit or
stand on. With legs dangling, the pilot comes as
close to being a bird as humanly possible.

Let's go hang gliding with Gilbert Aldrich, an
experienced hang-glider pilot who took the ride of
his life — and what could have been the ride of his
death.

It was a typical North Carolina summer afternoon, very hot with very little wind, when Gilbert
Aldrich and his fiancée, Nancy, drove up Sauratown
Mountain to go hang gliding. "A little still for this
July day, but perfect for flying," thought Gilbert as
they made their way to the launching site, past the
thick forest and up the steep slope to the top of the
mountain.

Gilbert and Nancy were meeting their friend Jim
Burton, who was another pilot and a fellow member
of the hang-gliding club to which they belonged.
Although Nancy had taken only a few courses in
the sport, Gilbert and Jim were old pros, and
between the two, there was plenty of experience
flying hang gliders.

As in any sport — especially one with the potential for danger, like flying — there is a specific way
to prepare before starting. Hang-glider pilots, in

particular, are very careful when getting ready for a flight, because there is so little equipment keeping them in the air. One small mistake, and there is no protection between the pilot and the ground hundreds of feet below. It is a long — and deadly — way down.

Wearing a helmet is another important safety feature, and the first thing the pilot does when preparing to go is attach his helmet to the crossbar so he won't forget it later — the helmet is put on right before takeoff. After making sure the hang glider is set properly, the pilot hooks himself into the equipment, which helps to keep his body flat rather than have his legs dangle straight down, flapping in the wind. And although the pilot does hold on to the crossbar, it really is used only to steer, not to keep from falling. The harness is what helps keep the pilot secure in the hang glider and safe from an unexpected — and dangerous — fall.

On this summer afternoon, Gilbert followed his pre-flight routine perfectly while Nancy helped him set up the hang glider. After carefully checking everything, Gilbert got in place for takeoff. Another hang-gliding expert and friend, Doug Rice, arrived at this time, planning to enjoy the sun and sky with the other pilots.

Jim had just flown off the launching pad, gracefully soaring from the mountaintop in the hazy sunshine. Gilbert hoped to be close behind. As Gilbert moved forward for his turn, Nancy realized he was not wearing his helmet. Gilbert, too, noticed this and tried to reach out and grab it before he left the ground.

The helmet was in a position just out of Gilbert's reach. He knew he needed to wear the headgear, so he unhooked himself from the hang glider — for just a second — to stretch as far as he could and grasp the helmet. As he placed it on his head, he was still in the position for takeoff — and still unhooked. As Nancy looked over at her fiancé, she noticed he had not secured himself back into his equipment. And with the breeze kicking up, it looked as if he might be leaving the ground soon!

Gilbert felt a gust of wind coming, and he and his hang glider were carried up and away, over the edge of the mountain and into the brilliant blue sky. But he was not hooked into the safety harness. He was hanging on for dear life.

Nancy could see he was in danger. His body was dangling straight down from the glider — this definitely was not the correct position. Growing increasingly nervous, Nancy screamed for help immediately. Her only hope for him was that he could keep a tight grip on the crossbar. If not, he would plummet to the dense forest below.

Watching with wide-eyed terror, Nancy could see Gilbert speeding down toward the trees. He was clearly in danger now, and there was no way for Nancy to get to him to help him. He bounced around as the hang glider dove faster and faster, banking off trees before landing out of sight in the woods.

Screaming out to Doug, who was preparing his equipment at his truck a few yards away, Nancy pointed out Gilbert's landing site. Almost unable to speak, Nancy was so upset that she forgot to tell Doug that Gilbert hadn't been strapped in. Doug thought his friend had just taken a wrong turn and misjudged his landing. He assured Nancy that he would be walking out of the forest in no time, laughing at himself for missing the ground.

Doug called out to Jim, who was still gliding through the air, to ask if he could see where Gilbert had landed. Jim did not see anything, so he and Doug agreed to meet down where they suspected Gilbert had landed.

Doug and Nancy looked down to the site and could see a figure walking among the trees. They thought this must be Gilbert, and, sighing with relief, they felt their friend must be okay. Doug joked to Nancy that Gilbert's biggest problem would be getting his huge hang glider out of a tree!

Driving separately down the mountain, Doug and Nancy headed with concern but less worry for the spot where they thought they had seen Gilbert walking. But as Doug approached the spot, there was no sign of Gilbert, or of anyone. He could see the hang glider in the trees, but no pilot could be found. Concern now turned into fear as Doug and Jim, who had landed near the site, followed a road leading to the hang glider. As they neared the area, they spotted Gilbert — lying on the ground, forty feet below the hanging hang glider. He was hurt.

Curled up on his left side, Gilbert was conscious but, having fallen all the way from the treetop, was very seriously injured. The two men had both taken a first-aid class and knew they could not move him, in case of any broken bones or internal wounds. But there was blood everywhere, and they were worried about this dangerous sign. Gilbert could move his legs, and at one point, he even tried to get up. But Jim and Doug knew, even if Gilbert didn't, that he was hurt badly and must stay where he was until help could arrive.

Removing his helmet and checking him over for injuries, they thought he had broken his elbow and might possibly have a concussion, or head injury. They had no idea what kind of injuries he had suffered inside his body, but they tried to make him as comfortable as they could.

Doug hurried off down the mountain to find a phone and get immediate emergency help for his hurt friend. He went to the first house he saw and dialed perhaps the three most important numbers in his — and Gilbert's — life: 911. Volunteer emergency medical technicians, or EMTs, from the Sauratown Volunteer Fire Department were sent out immediately to the emergency site. Greg Collins and Thomas Gordon, EMT paramedics from the Stokes County department, were also on their way after one quick telephone call. Doug waited at the bottom of the road to lead the emergency team to the accident.

Meanwhile, Nancy had driven down the mountain, still thinking Gilbert was fine. When she couldn't see any sign of him, or of Jim or Doug for that matter, she became frightened and felt for sure something must be wrong. She was near the home of a hang-gliding pilot, a man named "June Bug," who lived near the site and often helped other pilots when they were in trouble or just needed a hand. The two drove toward the hang glider, which they could see dangling from a tree. As they were climbing back up the road toward the accident site, Nancy could hear the scream of sirens, and she knew they were headed for Gilbert.

Nancy was on the verge of hysteria now as she drove ever faster to reach her fiancé. She arrived at the same time as the rescuers and, seeing so many emergency workers, thought the worst had happened. And where was Gilbert? She couldn't even see him; he was surrounded by busy and efficient EMTs.

Doug and Jim, seeing Nancy, rushed to her side to reassure her that Gilbert was indeed alive. He was, however, very badly hurt, they warned her. The three watched helplessly as the EMT crew and paramedics sprang into action.

The EMTs, skilled in dealing with emergencies in this mountainous area, quickly strapped Gilbert into a Stokes basket, which is like a stretcher — only more secure, so it can transport an injured person down a steep area safely without much movement. Once secured, Gilbert was transported out of the wooded area and into the back of a pickup truck, which drove him to an ambulance. Paramedic Greg Collins recognized that Gilbert's injuries would require treatment at the nearest hospital — and quickly. The only way to save Gilbert was to take him by helicopter to Baptist Hospital in Winston-Salem, an eight-minute helicopter ride. Greg had already called ahead for the copter, and it was waiting at the bottom of the mountain for Gilbert when he arrived.

Gilbert had not been able to fly his hang glider that afternoon, but in a rush of wind and thunder of propellers, Gilbert took to the sky now, strapped into the emergency helicopter that was speeding him to the hospital. Dr. Wayne Meredith met Gilbert in the emergency room and quickly and accurately identified his injuries. Dr. Meredith told Gilbert he needed immediate surgery — the doctor would have to open him up to repair the injuries inside.

Gilbert had a collapsed lung, a torn kidney, a broken elbow, and minor head injuries. Considering his terrible fall, it was not as bad as it might have been. But lung and kidney injuries can be very painful and very dangerous — even life-threatening. And Gilbert needed a major operation to fix the damaged organs.

The operation took five hours and was successful. Gilbert had to stay in the hospital for another eight weeks, half of which he doesn't even remember because of his head injuries. Nancy stayed by his side day and night, and when he was finally sent home, she stayed with him and nursed him through the long recuperation.

The swift, professional response to Doug's call to 911 saved Gilbert's life. Nancy and Gilbert both give total credit to the fast and efficient care these emergency volunteers provided on that mountaintop and to the quick-thinking assistance of Jim and Doug, who knew to call 911 immediately.

During his long journey back to health — an entire year — Gilbert did a lot of thinking. Although the sport of hang gliding was very exciting, he realized he could have died out there and he knew nothing was worth that. He certainly didn't want to put Nancy through that harrowing experience again — ever. Gilbert gave up hang gliding. And he is glad.

So is Nancy. She wanted Gilbert to stay with her for a long, long time. As horrible as the accident was, it did bring the two even closer together. In April 1991, Nancy and Gilbert were married, and now they enjoy the great outdoors together — this time from the ground, on mountain bikes. Gilbert will leave flying to the birds from now on.

☆☆☆

Amazing Facts

Did you know:

- People began flying more than 200 years ago — in hot-air balloons, that is!

- The first successful flight of an airplane — with wings and a motor — is credited to two Americans, Orville and Wilbur Wright, in 1903!

- The fastest airliner, the Concorde, travels at a speed of up to Mach 2.2 — or 1,450 miles per hour — and once flew from New York to London, England, in a record 2 hours, 55 minutes, and 15 seconds!

- People can now travel into space in an airplanelike rocket known as a Space Shuttle!

☆☆☆

Desert Flood

★ ★ ☆

White, flaky snow at Christmastime is a dream come true in the northern part of the United States. And mild, sunny days are thought of as "just right" for the winter holiday festivities in the South. This country is very large, and there's something different everywhere you go.

We've got deserts in the Southwest and wet forests in the Northwest and swampy bayous way down south. You can expect a tornado or two in the Midwest at certain times of the year, and a hurricane along the southeastern coast at other times. And earthquakes in California are fairly common. These weather changes are all part of nature, and while they may not be easy to predict, they usually happen in the same places over and over again.

But nothing is ever certain. Sometimes you get a mild earthquake in New York or maybe a snowstorm in Georgia. The unexpected doesn't happen often — but it can happen.

And it did happen recently in the southwestern state of Arizona — a beautiful state in the middle of a desert, which is well known for its sunshine and clear air. If you live in Arizona, you know how to keep cool on hot days and how to keep from getting thirsty in the very dry air. What you don't know much about is rain. It doesn't rain often, and never for very long. So if you lived in Arizona, you probably would never encounter a flood caused by rain. Or would you?

Ngan Tran certainly didn't expect a flood when she was driving home alone on August 22, 1992. Heavy rains had been falling for the past couple of days, which is very unusual in this desert area. Ms. Tran had no way of knowing how bad it could get, but she did notice that many of the roads seemed to be filling with water. She kept driving.

A road crossing what is normally a dry stream bed was blocked off with a police barricade — or barrier — to keep cars from traveling through. The rains had caused the stream bed to fill up, and now water was cascading across the road as if it were a newly formed river. The barricade had been set up to protect cars and their drivers from being swept away by these rushing waters.

As Ngan Tran approached the barricade, she was confused. She didn't understand that this barricade was meant to keep her and others off the flooding road. She needed to use this road to get to

her destination, and she was not going to turn
around now. She stepped on the gas and turned the
wheel. She drove around the barricade, not realizing the danger that lay ahead.

At first it was just a wet, splashy drive along a
slick road. The car would occasionally hydroplane
— or go out of control by skimming across the wet
surface — but she held tightly to the steering
wheel and continued ahead. The sky was still pour-
ing rain in the desert mountains, and the down-
stream washes were now swollen beyond their
banks. As Ngan Tran continued driving along the
blocked-off road, the flooding grew worse. Although the rain had lessened along this route, she
was beginning to realize that it was a serious mistake to have come this way.

Finally, her car could go no farther. The once dry
desert road was now a raging river, filling with
water faster and faster. Ms. Tran's car was hit by a
wave, then another. She stopped the car —
although the water had pretty much done that
already — and watched in horror as her car was
swept by the current off the main road. She was
now engulfed by the growing flood.

A motorist passing along the main road nearby
had noticed the car drive around the barricade and
checked to see where it had gone. Now, squinting
her eyes against the splashing water whipped up
by the wind, the motorist could barely see the top
of the car and the headlights. It was going to be
underwater soon! And there was still someone in

Ms. Tran's car was engulfed by the growing flood.

it! She reached for her mobile telephone and called
911.

Nearly hysterical, she told the 911 dispatcher
that a car had washed off the road and was nearly
underwater. The headlights were now under the
growing river and the person inside the car needed
help immediately. The police were dispatched right
away.

Arriving on the scene only moments later, the
police could see the top of the car in the middle of
the flood — and nothing more. A person was
trapped in the car, and their first thought was that
whoever it was could not survive for long. They
had to get to work immediately.

A police helicopter arrived just then and shone

its high-beam light onto the car; they could see the woman trapped inside. As long as she stayed put, there was a chance they could save her. If she tried to open the door and climb out into the raging waters, she would be swept away and drowned. They could only hope she wouldn't try to escape the car.

The helicopter belonged to the Phoenix Police Department's Air Support Unit, and this was co-pilot Sally Scott's first swift-water rescue. Her first concern was for the woman inside the car: How much air did she have? How much water was in the car? There was very little time to get her out before the car itself was washed away by the flood.

It was after 11:00 P.M., and the wind was picking up. The rescue was going to be difficult; now they had to attempt it in the dark. A second helicopter with a rescue-certified pilot was brought in to execute this delicate but crucial rescue.

Ron Cummings, a member of the swift-water rescue team, was dispatched to the scene and would join the helicopter crew to attempt a daring and unpredictable rescue. Ron would have to ride out on the helicopter skids and be set on top of the car. It would be his job to get the woman out and bring her back aboard the helicopter to safety. It was a very risky plan, and they didn't know if it would work. But they had to try something — and it had to be now.

Ron waited as the huge helicopter lowered itself to a point close enough for him to jump. The thun-

dering helicopter propellers were deafening, and
Ron had to scream to make himself heard. He
waited for the signal from the pilot to let him know
when it was safe to go. Ron needed to keep his
hands free to save Ms. Tran, so he had to leave the
safety flotation equipment — which is used to keep
people above the water — aboard the copter.

Slowly, steadily, the helicopter lowered Ron
toward the car. Attached to the helicopter by only a
safety cable and standing on the copter's skids,
Ron was soaking wet. Inch by inch, Ron was lowered onto the roof of the car, which was almost completely covered with water. As Ron landed on the
roof, his feet slipped and he swayed, nearly falling
headlong into the rapidly swirling waters below.
After a moment, he regained his balance and was
now stable on the car roof.

With great care, Ron leaned over, broke the back
window of the car, and helped Ms. Tran out, while
the helicopter overhead returned to him to drop off
the flotation equipment. This time around, the
helicopter had to get as close as possible to Ron and
the car so the equipment could be reached. The
helicopter was a large, loud, and not very graceful
machine. Between the wind and the tiny little tar-
get they were aiming for, the helicopter pilot had a
tough job maneuvering his copter back to the car. If
it were too far away, Ron wouldn't be able to reach
the safety equipment; if it were too close, the copter
would knock the rescuer and victim into the dangerous water.

Ron grabbed the life vest and put it on Ms. Tran. Rescuer and victim were now two shadows against the flood of lights from the two helicopters. They stood shakily upon the slick, slippery car roof, waiting to be rescued. The wind was stirred up by the propellers of the helicopter and the water lapped up along the edge of the car's roof, rising higher and higher, threatening to pull them down. It would be just minutes before the car disappeared under the river — and the two people with it.

The first few rescue attempts were disasters. Each time Ron reached out to touch the helicopter skids, they were just out of his grasp or he received a shock from the static charge built up by the

Rescuer and victim now waited, two shadows against the flood of lights from the two helicopters.

whirring blades. Each failed attempt meant the helicopter had to move away and try again to get close enough for the rescue.

Finally, after about the fifth try, Ron was able to securely take hold of the helicopter skids. Holding them steady, he stepped onto the skids and pulled Ms. Tran up with him. They were both out of danger and thankful to be alive.

Looking down at the scene below, Ron could see the water completely envelop the car. Later, the pressure of the flooding waters pushed the car out of its precarious spot. In one sweep, the car was gone, washed away by the rapids.

Ngan Tran had been trapped in her water-bound car for over an hour. Imagine the terror, the desperation she felt as she looked out her windows and saw the rising level of water surrounding her. In the darkness, she was alone and isolated and had no way to communicate with the outside world. She didn't know if she would be saved or if she would drown. She did not even know how to swim. There was no escape.

The real reason Ms. Tran may have survived, however, was ironic: she *didn't* know how to swim. She knew she could not attempt to get out of the car and swim to safety, so she stayed put, waiting for help to arrive. Had she tried to climb out through a window, rescuers agree, she would have been quickly and violently swept away by the raging flood. Swimming would not have helped her at all, because she would have been powerless to fight the current.

Thanks to the quick-thinking motorist along the road, 911 dispatchers were able to evaluate the situation and send the right emergency crew to rescue Ms. Tran. The courageous team of pilots and rescuers pushed themselves to the limit to make this rescue a success. They worked as a team, each with a specific and important job that had to be done. And they did it — even at those tense moments when they didn't think they could.

Today, Ms. Tran and her ten-year-old daughter are forever grateful to these brave men and women. Ms. Tran was particularly impressed with the way these people pulled together and really cared about rescuing her. Her faith in people was renewed. Her daughter gives credit to the rescue team for their heroic efforts under extremely difficult circumstances. They saved her mom, and to her that is about the most important thing in the world.

Ms. Tran advises everyone who drives to pay attention to road signs, barricades, and signals. They are put there for a reason — for your own safety. If she had not ignored the barricade blocking the flooded road, she never would have been caught on the verge of death. She will never again dismiss those important signs. And she hopes none of you will either.

☆☆☆

Amazing Facts

Did you know:

- Every year there are about 500,000 earthquakes that can be detected. Around 100,000 can actually be felt, and 1,000 of those can cause damage!

- The North and South Poles have the least amount of sunshine in the world — 182 days without sun in the South Pole; 176 days in the North Pole!

- During one hailstorm in the country of Bangladesh, hailstones weighed up to $2\frac{1}{4}$ pounds each!

- The coldest place in the world is in Antarctica at a place called the Pole of Cold, where the average annual temperature is $-72°F$!

☆☆☆

Three Men and a Little Girl

★ ★ ☆

Spending time with family and friends is a great way to relax, have fun, and really get to know the people you love. An afternoon in the park flying kites, an exciting day at the amusement park (complete with a roller-coaster ride!), or a pickup game of ball helps to bring people closer together.

And even though a family outing is a time to forget about your troubles and just have fun, you must never forget to be careful. Danger can lurk in the most innocent places. Don't let yourself be fooled. A beautiful sunny day can suddenly turn dark and stormy; a friendly-looking animal might unexpectedly turn mean; a calm pool of water may hide a strong, deadly current that can sweep anything — and anybody — away in a split second.

The Martinez family — Ruth and her two daughters, Camillia and Anna — learned a valuable lesson in caution. But not before they lived through a nightmare of terror and won an almost impossible battle for survival.

Ruth Martinez and her daughters often went on family outings together. They liked to take time out from work, homework, and chores as often as possible to go on special family trips to all different places. The threesome loved to play and relax with each other on a lazy afternoon. It was on one such afternoon that the Martinez family discovered how quickly safe surroundings can turn dangerous, how a dreamy day can suddenly become a nightmare.

June 11, 1991 was a sunny, pleasant, ideal day for the family to enjoy the scenery of the Colorado Rocky Mountains. Ruth took ten-year-old Camillia, six-year-old Anna, and Anna's young friend to the peaceful shores of Clear Creek in Golden, Colorado, for a day of play. And that is exactly how the trip began.

The creek seemed calm and beautiful; not a ripple spoiled its clean, clear surface. But there was a steady current. Surrounded by the majestic mountains, the spot Ruth had chosen for the outing was quiet, private, and pretty, even though there was a popular campsite nearby.

Sitting along the shore, Ruth watched as her children and their friend skimmed rocks across the water, counting the skips they made with each toss. Feeling the water tentatively, Anna discovered it was ice cold — certainly not the kind of water to go swimming in today, but not too bad for just splashing along the shore.

Ruth sat back to read a good book, keeping an eye on the kids and telling them not to go too far into the water. The peals of laughter and sound of splashing assured Ruth that the children were having fun.

But in the mountains, the calm appearance of a river or stream can be very deceiving — it is almost never what it seems. Under the smooth surface, there is usually a very strong — often deadly — current that moves so swiftly it can carry even the largest man away before he knows what is happening. The power of these calm-looking waterways must be respected and never be underestimated. Although Clear Creek looked harmless, even shallow, the Martinez family had no idea what lay beneath the surface — yet.

Camillia left the two younger children to go play on their own, a little farther away. As Camillia walked along the shore, she became more curious — and more courageous — and decided to go deeper into the creek. Slowly, she waded through the icy chill, water lapping at her ankles, then her knees, and, soon, her thighs.

As Camillia walked, she realized that the creek was not quite as shallow as it appeared. She also noticed that there was a strong pull under the water, forcing her legs to shift every time she tried to lift them. Continuing for another step or two, Camillia was suddenly plunged into very deep water, the freezing cold wetness soaking her clothes and, soon, her face. She clung to a nearby

Camilla struggled to hold on to a rock, but she was beginning to lose her battle with the strong current.

rock, but found it hard to hang on. The current
seemed to want to drag her away, drag her down.

Ruth, who was keeping an eye on the two
younger children, saw Camillia a short distance
out in the creek. She called for her to come back
into the shore — today was no day for swimming.
At first, it was hard for Ruth to tell what was happening to her daughter. She didn't look as if she
was too far out; perhaps she was just fooling
around. Calling out again to quit kidding and
return to the banks, Ruth looked closer. Her
daughter looked like she was struggling to hold on
to the rock. Then she was gone!

Camillia had gone under the water for only a
moment, but she was already beginning to lose her

battle with the strong current. Ruth sprang into
action, seeing that her little girl was in very serious danger. Jumping into the frigid waters, Ruth
swam hard to reach Camillia before the frightened
girl went under again. She reached the rock and
tried desperately to free Camillia and take her
back to shore. But the creek was far stronger than
the brave mother.

"The water felt like a vacuum sucking my feet,
and I just lost it," Ruth remembered. Neither she
nor her daughter could keep their grip on the rock,
their last chance at safety. Along the shore, Anna
and her friend screamed hysterically, fearing the
mother and child would drown in the swiftly moving water.

Ruth and Camillia were swept away, pried loose
from the rock and down the creek, swirling and
bobbing in the rapid currents of Clear Creek.

Ruth lost hold of Camillia, was pulled under
briefly, then managed to get out and run along the
bank. She met a man who was riding a bike, and he
called 911 from a campground. As it happened, the
police headquarters were located right along the
banks of Clear Creek. Detectives Stan Ross and
Glenn Moore of the Golden Police Department
heard the call and rushed out to respond.

They were doubtful that anyone could survive a
fall in the creek because of the condition of the
water at that time of year. In the spring, melting
snow runs off the mountains, and by summertime,
the creeks and rivers become full. Full and forceful.

The two officers feared that, even if they found her, they would not be rescuing a live girl but pulling a body out of the water.

As they approached the water, both men admitted to each other that they were not very good swimmers. With a nervous laugh, they promised they would save each other if the "going got rough" — which they fully expected.

What they didn't expect was to find the girl alive or to have to wrestle her from the violent clutches of the rain-swollen creek.

Ruth watched helplessly, painfully, as her older daughter continued to be carried farther and farther away by the swirling waters.

Back at police headquarters, Commander Bill Kilpatrick also heard the radio dispatch for the emergency at Clear Creek. Being very familiar with the area and that particular creek, he knew that time could not be wasted. If the call had come in thirty to forty-five seconds later, the rescue team never would have had a chance of even seeing the girl. They would have been too late.

From the banks, the two officers spotted Camillia, moving so swiftly now that it was hard to keep her in sight. Without hesitation — without even thinking — Officers Ross and Moore leaped into the cold Colorado creek to rescue the little girl. Thinking they would swim out and grab her, the men were taken by complete surprise when they lost control themselves. Once they were in the water, the creek had a mind of its own, pulling and tearing at the two strong men as if they were rag dolls.

Officer Ross felt as if someone had "grabbed his legs and pulled" him underwater. He couldn't fight it. He, too, began the quick, frightening ride along the current, tossed about like a leaf in high wind. If the brave police officer was this scared, he could only imagine what the drowning child must be feeling. Realizing that he was in serious danger himself, Officer Ross knew he had to save himself before he could be any help in saving the girl. Finally, catching his balance and keeping afloat, Officer Ross found the strength to assist in the rescue.

Officer Moore had been luckier in fighting the current and was able to reach Camillia. But the current continued to pull mightily, and he was having difficulty keeping the girl's head above water. Each time he succeeded in lifting the girl up, his own head submerged in the icy water.

Stan Ross got his bearings and, spotting Officer Moore and Camillia, struggled to their side. Together, the men battled the raging currents to drag the victim, ever so slowly, to shore. Once they did, there was no time for relief or recovery for the men, however. When Camillia was dragged out, they discovered she was unconscious. She did not cough, she didn't even move. The two officers feared the worst, but they continued to pull her up onto the bank for closer inspection.

By this time, the men realized that the girl was

not breathing; nor did she have a pulse. Trying to
empty the child's lungs of water, Officers Ross and
Moore discovered that the bank was very steep and
bumpy. They needed to get Camillia to a firm, flat
spot to begin CPR — or cardiopulmonary resuscita-
tion, in which the heart and lungs of a victim with
no pulse or breathing are "restarted" by a combina-
tion of massage and mouth-to-mouth breathing.
For this procedure to be effective, the victim must
be lying flat and the person who is giving CPR
must be consistent and not be interrupted. Once
the officers start, they must keep going if they are
to save her.

Moving the heavy, waterlogged girl up the steep
slope was almost impossible. Both men were completely exhausted from their own struggles with
the creek. Slipping and falling, the officers were
beginning to think they could never make it when,
out of nowhere, Commander Kilpatrick arrived on
the scene. Using all his considerable strength,
Commander Kilpatrick pushed all three people up
the hill to safe and level ground.

Although she had been submerged underwater
for so long, the men felt the girl might just have a
chance. This was because the water was so cold,
and extremely cold water slows down the body's
functions — like heart rate and breathing — so
that it needs less oxygen and blood flow. Although
her heart had stopped and she was not breathing,
the low body temperature might actually protect
her from serious damage.

At the campground near Clear Creek, Ruth and the two younger children waited anxiously for some news of Camillia. When an ambulance came screaming up, lights flashing, Ruth flagged down the paramedics and pleaded with them to take her along with them. Climbing into the back, Ruth, Anna, and her friend raced along in the ambulance to find Camillia.

The three men and the little girl were at the top of the embankment. Physically and emotionally drained, the police officers would not give up on saving this young girl, a child who reminded Officer Ross of his own daughter. It was a miracle that they had even found her. They would not let her die.

Commander Kilpatrick flagged down the arriving rescue squad, who appeared on the scene just in time. They were like a relay team, ready to take over just as the exhausted officers reached the final limits of their energy. CPR was continued on Camillia by the newly arrived rescuers.

Standing back from the drama, the three men looked at each other in a kind of daze. Now that the first danger had been resolved, the child's life and future were still at stake. How long had she been in the water? How long had she gone without oxygen? And how would this affect her brain?

When Foothills Ambulance paramedic Dana Hollingsworth arrived on the scene, Camillia still had no pulse and was not breathing. He had seen other drowning victims, caught in the water for

just as long as the young girl, who had not survived. He did not know what to expect for the
deathly still child, but he was going to do everything in his power to try to save her.

Getting out of the paramedic ambulance, Ruth
and the two younger children remained by the road
a good distance from Camillia and the frantic rescue attempts. Ruth was terrified, and watching her
daughter lie motionless would only make it worse
for her and the workers. Unable to do anything
else, she clung to the children, looking out at the
mountains, and prayed.

Finally, a sign of life! The paramedics were able
to start Camillia's heart! She was then immediately rushed to Lutheran Medical Center nearby
and examined by Emergency-Room physician Dr.
Carla Murphy.

Dr. Murphy noted that the girl's body temperature was 83.6°F whereas a normal temperature is
98.6°F. This was a good sign, because while the
cold is slowing down the body functions, it also
reduces the need for oxygen. But the doctor was
still not hopeful — Camillia's breathing was very
shallow and she was not responding at all. She was
in a coma. The doctor expected her to stay that way
until she died.

Ruth didn't understand the serious nature of her
daughter's condition. Whether she *could* not or
would not believe the doctor, Ruth never gave up
hope that her daughter would fully recover. While
leaning over her beloved child in the Emergency

Room, Ruth saw a small drop of water — what she believed was a tear — trickle down Camillia's cheek. She felt a warm, close bond with her child at that moment and never doubted that her little girl would make it.

Camillia was transferred to Children's Hospital in Denver in a deep coma. For the next three days and nights, Ruth kept a constant vigil over her daughter, waiting for a sign that she would regain consciousness. On the third day, she was rewarded.

While holding Camillia's hand, Ruth leaned closer and heard a whisper. It was Camillia trying to speak. She said, "God."

"What?" her mother asked gently.

"God sent me back," was the quiet but firm reply. Camillia had truly come back.

Everyone involved in this amazing rescue believes Camillia's recovery is a miracle. Looking at Camillia today, it is not hard to believe.

Although she had to learn to do everything — even walk — all over again, Camillia is a normal, active twelve-year-old girl who likes to play with her little sister and help her mother. She is most grateful to her heroes — the three men who rescued her.

Officers Ross and Moore and Commander Kilpatrick were honored for heroism by the Standing Rock Sioux Tribe and the Golden Police Department and can be tremendously proud of a job well done.

But their greatest reward has been the apprecia-

Officers Ross and Moore and Commander Kilpatrick saved Camillia's life. Her mother and sister will always be grateful for their bravery.

tion of the Martinez family and the gratification they feel for their own efforts in giving young Camillia her life back.

That is the true reward.

☆☆☆

Amazing Facts

Did you know:

- The longest anyone has ever remained in a coma is thirty-seven years!
- Three teams each performed CPR continuously for more than 120 hours in a marathon!
- A man once swam down the Mississippi River for a total of 1,826 miles — and he was in the water for 742 hours!

☆☆☆

Lady's No Tramp

☆ ☆ ☆

Do you have a hero? Someone you really look up to or whom you feel is extra special? Superman, Batman, a favorite teacher, or, of course, Mom and Dad can all be heroes to many of us. We can admire their courage and strength — not only the kind of strength superheroes use to destroy the villains, but the kind that comes from doing the right thing and helping solve a difficult problem. We can learn from our heroes and try to be like them ourselves.

A hero can come in any shape or size. He or she doesn't even have to be human — or a cartoon character, for that matter. And the heroic deed is not always something that is planned. Sometimes, being a hero is as surprising to the hero as being in danger is to a potential victim.

You are about to meet one of the most impressive

heroes you will ever know. Although she is only nine years old, she is strong, fast, and very brave. She wasn't trying to be a hero, but her love for her family made her jump into action without a second thought. Her own safety was not her concern; she was saving another's life. This hero, by the way, is a dog.

It all happened on Labor Day, 1992, in Larimer County, Colorado, when an innocent family picnic turned into a nightmare in a split second. Nestled in the beautiful Rocky Mountains, Larimer County is one of the most breathtaking examples of the miracle of nature. Open fields surrounded by trees, a bubbling creek dividing the land — the area was the perfect spot for Richard and Oma Thomson to build their dream home. It was also the perfect spot for nature's creatures — those that fly overhead *and* those that slither on the ground.

The Thomsons took a ride out to the area for a holiday barbecue with their four grandchildren — Rachel, age nine; Teresa, eight; Audrey, seven; and five-year-old David. Also packed into the family truck for the outing were the four family dogs, including a beautiful nine-year-old retriever/husky mix named Lady.

As the Thomsons pulled up to the site of their future home, their daughter Sandra arrived with plenty of hot dogs and buns to join in the fun. As the cars were being unpacked, the Thomsons' other daughter, Laura, and her husband, Bob Martinez — parents of Teresa, Audrey, and David — pulled

in. Together, the large clan grabbed the groceries
and began their hike to the barbecue pit and the
party.

The day was warm and sunny — perfect for a
long, giggling game of tag or the take-turns excitement of the rope swing. Squealing and laughing,
the children played noisily while the adults took
their time unpacking and preparing the afternoon
cookout. The family was together, and the adults
were happy to talk and joke and watch their children and grandchildren enjoy the day.

Around four o'clock that afternoon, the kids
decided they were getting hungry. The grown-ups
agreed it was about time to eat, and they prepared
to light the barbecue. Seven-year-old Audrey
announced that she had to go to the bathroom.
With that, all the other kids, and some of the
adults too, realized that they also had to relieve
themselves.

Because the house was not yet built and there
was no bathroom around for miles, the family used
an area they called "the latrine," which was really
just an area located in the bushes and trees safely
away from the barbecue pit. A small creek sepa-
rated the areas where the boys and girls went to
the bathroom, so Grandma Oma took Audrey and
Rachel by the hand, with Teresa following behind,
while Bob and David went to the other side of the
creek.

Aunt Sandra went along with the girls, while
Grandpa Richard and Laura stayed behind to cook

the hot dogs. Lady, not a very active dog to begin
with, stayed behind with them, happy to rest lazily
while everyone was busy with some activity or
other.

Back by the creek, Teresa was still in a playful
mood, and she dashed ahead to the latrine before
the others could catch up. She disappeared behind
the shrubs as the rest of the group approached the
latrine at a more leisurely pace.

Suddenly, a strange and scary sound filled the
still afternoon air. It was a rattling noise, a noise
that sent shivers down the spines of everyone who
could hear it. It was the sound of rattlesnakes —
not just one but many. And they were all around
the girl out in the middle of the bushes — far from
the safety of the barbecue pit.

Shocked and horrified, the two women stopped
in their tracks and looked around quietly and carefully. Rattlesnakes are among the most dangerous
types of snake, and their bite is poisonous — and
deadly. The dry, loose segment at the end of a rattler's tail produces a strange rattling sound when
he shakes it, giving the snake his name. The sound
can be a warning, but Grandma Oma and Aunt
Sandra knew the snakes must be dangerously close
by, because they could hear it so clearly. And they
also knew that any sudden move can cause the
snake to strike out and bite. Rattlers are very
quick, and they usually hit what they're aiming for.

Afraid for her granddaughter Teresa, who was
hidden behind the bushes, Grandma Oma called

out for her to be still. She warned of the rattlesnakes and told the girl not to move. Looking
around in alarm, young Teresa spotted a big rattler
glaring up at her from a nest just a few steps away.
Screaming and nearly frozen with panic, Teresa
shouted to her grandmother that she had discovered a whole lot of deadly snakes.

Knowing she had to keep the child calm,
Grandma Oma again encouraged Teresa to keep
still and told her help was on the way. It is important to avoid any sudden movement when con-
fronted by a rattlesnake. The snake is much faster
than you and, without warning, will strike out and
possibly hurt you very seriously. Grandma Oma
knew there was very little time before the scared
child would try to run away and, possibly, cause the
rattler to bite her. Oma called out frantically to the
others at the barbecue pit. "Come quick," she cried,
"there's rattlers all around us."

Suddenly, alerted to the possibility of danger,
Lady jumped up from her lazy nap and sprang into
action. Before the others even realized what was
happening, Lady had raced across the field and
into the bushes, looking to protect her friend
Teresa. As Lady approached the spot, a large rattler lashed out at the dog, barely missing her with
its ugly fangs.

This only served to make Lady even more angry,
and she bared her own teeth, growling and snap-
ping at the reptile. Seeing her chance to escape,
Teresa ran through the trees to stand beside her

grandmother and aunt. All were shaking badly from the close call, but no one had been harmed.

In the bushes, Lady continued to fight as the frightened family looked on. Grandma Oma watched in horror as the largest rattler coiled up like a spring and lashed out at Lady, striking her above the eye. Recoiling, the snake struck again, this time on the side of the brave dog's face.

By this time, the children, crying hysterically and very shaken, were safely back with the rest of the family. Now their concern was for Lady. Bob and Laura, Teresa's parents, called desperately to Lady to come back and get away from the danger. At first, Lady didn't respond. She continued to fight like a wild animal, protecting her loved ones from a terrible enemy. In the next moment, however, Lady stopped her fighting and looked around cautiously, assuring herself that her family was safe from harm. When she was sure everyone was all right, Lady turned and walked away from the raging rattler.

Looking exhausted, Lady walked slowly toward the others at the barbecue pit. Cheering on their hero, the family excitedly waited to congratulate Lady on her courageous fight and brave rescue. But Lady slumped to the ground, more than just tired. She looked hurt. She looked ill. Had she been bitten by her enemy?

Grandma Oma remembered seeing Lady get struck by the snake, and quickly they examined the dog closely. They discovered two puncture

wounds above Lady's right eye — two holes made
by the fangs of the poison snake.

Moving with great speed, Oma and Laura placed
Lady in the car and drove off for help. Remember, a
rattlesnake bite can be very dangerous — and it
can kill. Oma held Lady gently on her lap while
Laura raced through the dirt roads and over to a
neighbor's house to telephone the veterinarian, Dr.
Jerry Butts. Dr. Butts told Laura to take the dog to
a nearby veterinary hospital at Colorado State
University. Although the hospital was only fifteen
miles away, it was a holiday weekend, and traffic
was very slow and difficult. Struggling to remain
calm and get the dog medical treatment as fast as
possible, Laura drove surely and steadily through
the traffic until they reached the hospital.
Throughout the forty-five-minute trip, Oma
caressed the sick dog, keeping an ice pack over the
injury to try and ease the pain.

Once at the hospital, another veterinarian, Dr.
Lisa Metelman, and a student raced to meet the
car and bring Lady inside on a stretcher. Lady's
face was swollen to twice its normal size and she
was taken immediately to the critical-care unit,
where they discovered exactly what was wrong and
began treatment.

More than a half hour later, Dr. Metelman
returned to the lobby where Oma and Laura
waited anxiously for news. The doctor said Lady
had only a fifty-fifty chance of surviving the snake
bite. The dog needed a special dose of antivenin

serum — medicine to keep the poisonous snake venom from killing the animal — and Laura and Oma were sent on a mission to pick up two vials of the medicine at a nearby hospital.

Another thirty minutes passed before the women returned with the serum. Racing into the hospital, the women handed off the vials to Dr. Metelman, who swiftly ran to Lady's room and gave her a shot of the medicine. It was now two and a half hours after Lady had been bitten by the rattler. Would the serum work in time? Or had this brave dog given her life to save her young friend?

Oma and Laura left Lady at the hospital and returned home, where the rest of the family waited. During an emotional and tearful evening, the family explained to the children that Lady might die, but that even if she did, she was a very special dog, a brave and true friend who had saved Teresa's life. The entire family cried themselves to sleep that night.

Eager for news of their dog, Laura called the hospital first thing the next morning to see if the serum had worked. Dr. Steven Hill, who was on duty at the time, was happy to report that Lady had responded well to the medicine and she seemed to be improving steadily. By 5:00 P.M., the family was told they could bring their friend home. The sounds of excited screams and joyful tears were deafening, and the family was ecstatic as they drove to the hospital to get their Lady.

At first, it was hard to recognize Lady. She

looked older and tired. Her swollen face gave her
head a lopsided look, and much of the fur on her
head had been shaved. The bruises were still big
and painful looking where the fangs had pierced
her eyebrow.

Walking down the hospital corridor to greet their
dog, the children were excited, but also sorry to see
Lady looking so bad. Suddenly, Lady saw the children and perked up immediately, becoming the
Lady everyone knew and loved. She pulled at her
leash so hard that it almost snapped, and she tried
to run the entire length of the hall to greet her family. Doctors, nurses and family alike could hardly
believe this feisty dog had been on the verge of
death only hours before.

Lady is fine today, her usual playful — sometimes lazy — self. But even more, Lady is a hero,
and the Martinez and Thomson families will never
forget how this beloved animal put her life on the
line for those she loved.

☆☆☆

Amazing Facts

Did you know:

- Most snakes are not harmful or poisonous.

- A snake can dislocate, or unhook, its jaw to make its mouth big enough to swallow food much larger than itself.

- Rattlesnakes are mostly found in the West and Southwest of the United States and in many South American countries.

- The sound the rattler makes is caused by loosely attached, horny pieces of skin that make a buzz, or rattle, when the snake shakes them. The sound is also a warning to any potential victim — so pay attention to the rattlesnake when it rattles!

☆☆☆

From Real Life to "Reel" Life

Selecting the Stories for
Rescue 911

☆ ☆ ☆

Every minute of every day, calls come in to 911 dispatchers at emergency centers around the country. The dispatchers answer each and every call — from minor mishaps to critical, life-threatening emergencies — and send help as it is needed.

Every week, you can relive some of the most exciting, amazing rescues ever made by courageous emergency teams and rescue squads on the hit CBS Television series *Rescue 911*. Each episode is bursting with improbable disasters and impossible rescues. Parents, kids — even animals — become real-life heroes facing incredible, dangerous, and often life-or-death situations.

The most amazing thing about *Rescue 911* is that every show is based on real people's experiences. Many of the stories you see each week are taken directly from the actual 911 calls for help.

Imagine the millions of adventures and human dramas that are played out each year from Portland, Oregon, to Portland, Maine; from Springfield, Missouri, to Springfield, Massachusetts — and all points in between!

But with so many daring rescues and thousands of heroes, how does an emergency situation end up on national television on *Rescue 911*?

It takes many people doing many different jobs to make a hit TV show, and *Rescue 911* is a perfect example of this kind of teamwork. Researchers — whose job it is to track down exciting rescues for the show — are assigned their own specific parts of the country, what are called their "territories." Each researcher keeps track of his or her own territory, checking out 911 calls, police and fire departments, and other emergency services to see what kinds of rescues have been made recently. The researcher is also responsible for assessing newspaper reports of exciting and unusual rescues in his or her territory.

Advertisements are placed in some of the magazines read by emergency workers, asking them to send in their own interesting rescues for possible use on the show. And because *Rescue 911* is a popular series watched by millions, viewers will often contact the show directly with their own amazing experiences.

With the huge amounts of information compiled every day by researchers, the *Rescue 911* production team — which puts the show together each week — has more than enough material to choose from.

But how do they choose? What makes a rescue right for *Rescue 911*?

While just about every emergency story has elements of excitement and danger, it is impossible to use them all on television. There are several things the show's producers look for when deciding which rescues will make it to the screen, including:

- a good descriptive interview, with the people involved showing strong feelings about their rescue

- an interesting location or stunt, or a dangerous and exciting physical element to the story that will make a good visual picture for television

- a unique and unusual story or rescue that has never been featured on the show before

- a strong 911 phone connection — one or more calls that make the dispatcher and the person reporting the emergency vital parts of the rescue

After a suitable story has been identified by the researchers, it is described in detail, in writing, and given to the executive producer and his team of producers so that they can read and discuss every angle of the story. If this team agrees that the story is good, it is then sent to the segment producer, who is in charge of that story — or segment — of the show.

The story is again reviewed, this time more closely, to see if it can, in fact, be filmed accurately, dramatically and safely for television. If the segment producer discovers an unsolvable problem, the story is dropped and will not appear on the show. If there are no problems, the story is "green lighted," or approved, and it will then go into production.

A few months later, while you relax safely in your home and tune in to your favorite TV show, you will see that same amazing story come to life before your eyes ... on *Rescue 911*!

☆☆☆